Oxford**basics**

CROSS-CURRICULAR ACTIVITIES

See the Oxford University Press ELT website at
http://www.oup.com/elt for further details.

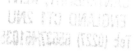

Oxford **basics**

Cross-curricular Activities

HANA ŠVECOVÁ

OXFORD

UNIVERSITY PRESS

OXFORD
UNIVERSITY PRESS

Great Clarendon Street, Oxford OX2 6DP

Oxford University Press is a department of the University of Oxford.
It furthers the University's objective of excellence in research, scholarship,
and education by publishing worldwide in

Oxford New York

Auckland Cape Town Dar es Salaam Hong Kong Karachi
Kuala Lumpur Madrid Melbourne Mexico City Nairobi
New Delhi Shanghai Taipei Toronto

With offices in

Argentina Austria Brazil Chile Czech Republic France Greece
Guatemala Hungary Italy Japan Poland Portugal Singapore
South Korea Switzerland Thailand Turkey Ukraine Vietnam

OXFORD and OXFORD ENGLISH are registered trade marks of
Oxford University Press in the UK and in certain other countries

ISBN-13: 978 0 19 442188 1

Printed in China

Contents

Introduction

When I became a teacher, I was convinced that the concept of cross-curricular links was invented to make a teacher's job miserable. I had the impression that cross-curricular teaching had very little relevance to what I was supposed to teach. I was sure there was no time for it in the packed syllabus and thought I was not qualified enough to work with cross-curricular topics. I was only an English teacher whose knowledge of other subjects was rather limited. Over the years, however, I began to realize that I did not have to be a scientific expert and that using cross-curricular topics made my lessons practical and motivating. What I thought was a burden proved to be a very good means of showing my learners that language is a great tool that enables us to exchange knowledge and opinions about the real world.

The benefits of cross-curricular activities

How can your learners benefit from cross-curricular activities? Cross-curricular activities:

- give learners a sense of how English and cross-curricular subjects fit together. They see how the knowledge and skills they have learned can be applied to English.
- encourage learners to work with topics so that they begin to see English as a means of communication and learning, not just a set of rules and list of words.
- motivate learners to explore topics, either themselves or with their classmates, or with their teacher – in English.
- give learners the opportunity to revise and consolidate their ability to use structures and vocabulary they have already studied.
- can help increase learners' self-confidence by giving them a chance to talk about what they have already learned or know from experience.
- offer learners meaningful topics to talk about. A choice of interesting and relevant cross-curricular topics can help prevent the situation in which your learners understand, for example, how to use a structure, but they do not use it because they are short of ideas and do not know what to say. Cross-curricular topics make the content clear and specific.
- help learners to see the relationship between the school curriculum and their real-life experiences.
- help learners to think and solve problems, speak to each other in pairs or groups, and develop communication and presentation skills.

The units

The book contains 30 activity-based lesson plans ready for teachers to use. The units work with topics selected from science, mathematics, biology, geography, history, drama, art, music, and literature, which are relevant to the learners' real-life experiences.

Who is the book for?

The book is a good resource for teachers who would like to apply ideas and strategies in their teaching which encourage communication. It can be successfully used in schools by teachers who only have a few resources and are looking for ways to make their lessons more interesting and motivating. The material is suitable for teachers who are just starting to develop their teaching skills, or who have little training, as well as teachers with more experience. The activities can be used with learners between elementary and intermediate levels in both small and larger classes. With the exception of very young learners, it is appropriate for all age groups.

When to use the book

The lessons are very flexible and can be used in a variety of ways, for example:

- as supplementary material for the cross-curricular element of a course
- as free-standing activities to develop learners' fluency and confidence in communicating
- as fun activities to provide variety to a course
- as a way to revise structures and vocabulary
- as ready-to-use material for cover lessons.

How to use the book

Each lesson plan starts with a short introduction to help you plan your lesson. The introduction contains the following:

Target language tells you what vocabulary, structure, or function is being introduced or practised in the unit.

Cross-curricular links informs you which cross-curricular subjects the unit is related to.

Resources lists all the resources and materials you are going to need to teach the lesson. You may need to prepare these before the lesson.

Preparation tells you what you should do before the lesson.

Time guide suggests how much time you need to teach the lesson. Most units are designed to last 45 minutes. As you probably know from your teaching experience, there are factors that may slow a lesson down or speed it up a little, such as how many learners you have in the class, what their general language level is, what time of the day you teach the class, whether the class are used to pair/group work, etc.

How to adapt the material

You are welcome to approach these units as frameworks from which you can develop your own lessons. Every group of learners is different and you may wish to adapt a unit to suit your particular class – their age, their language level, where you are teaching, where the learners are from, what they are interested in, what they need to study, and so on. This gives you control over the level of difficulty, both of the activity and the language, and over the topic and vocabulary area. Here are some ways of adapting the material:

- the topic of a unit or activity – the teaching ideas can often be adapted to other topics. For example, the 'Stone Age' lesson could also work with the Iron Age or the Middle Ages; different authors and books could be chosen for the 'Library' lesson; a different song could be used in 'Drawing a song'; different inventions and discoveries could be used in 'Tree rings', etc.
- the vocabulary area – you can also adapt the lessons to different vocabulary areas. For example, you could choose a different set of fruit or vegetables in 'Fruit and vegetables'; you could change the list of things to do in 'Timetable'; you could choose different situations for 'Multiplying and dividing', etc.
- the level of difficulty of vocabulary – you can add or take out more difficult words. For example, in 'Coat of arms' you can change the character words in stage 2 (for example, 'happy' for 'optimistic'); in 'Animals' you can take out the more difficult words like 'slither' and 'scales'; you could make the list of equipment in 'Weight' more difficult.
- the amount of vocabulary – you can cut or add to the amount of vocabulary in an activity, for example, the number of adjectives you introduce in 'Materials'.
- the structure – you can choose how much input and practice of a structure you give your learners. For example, in 'Plants' the target language is 'Does it …?', 'Do you …?', and 'Has it got …?'. You could write these on the board at the beginning of stage 6. You could also do an example in front of the class with a learner. You could drill the language. You could let the learners do the activity once and then put the target language on the board. You could let the learners do the activity without any input or practice. There are

lots of options available. You choose what you think will work best with your class.

- the level of difficulty of the activity – you can make the activity itself easier or more difficult. In 'Fractions', for example, the level of difficulty of mathematics can easily be changed.
- the sequence of the stages – some lesson plans contain ideas on how to vary the sequencing of activities. You can choose a variation that is more suitable for your class. You can also leave out some parts or stages from the unit completely and put in new material instead.
- the amount of text – you can increase or reduce the amount of text that you give the learners. For example, you could lengthen or shorten the example story in stage 1 of 'Multiplying and dividing'. You can do the same with stage 3 of 'Fractions'.
- the amount of explanation – you can give your learners information or you can ask them to tell you what they know. For example, in 'Plants' you give your learners information about the parts of different plants in stage 1. Alternatively you could draw the plants without an explanation and ask the learners what the different parts of the plant are called.

Resources

Some units contain hands-on activities that enable the learners to create, work with, or manipulate various objects and materials. This stimulates their motivation and helps the learning process. All the resources used in the activities should be easy for you to find. For example, in 'Sight' you provide metal spoons and mirrors for the learners to carry out some simple experiments. In 'Taste, touch, and smell' you can bring in samples of different materials to feel, and various tastes and smells you want the learners to sense. For 'Framed pictures' you will need simple props like a comb, umbrella, or chair you may find at school or even in the classroom. Many activities work only with essential resources, such as paper, pens, or pencils, and the board on which you can prepare simple drawings or texts before you start the class and work with later on in the lesson.

Helping learning

The activities often use games or drama techniques to motivate the learners. Strategies, such as miming or using gestures, not only assist the learners in class, they can also help them to make themselves understood in real life situations.

Playfulness and a fun element in language learning often make the process more enjoyable and effective. If your learners find an activity entertaining, there is a better chance they will learn and remember the language.

Some units work with simple pictures that are easy for you to copy on the board or paper cards. The learners sometimes use pictures or artwork in the activities to express what they know or how they understand the topic. Using simple drawings to record thoughts or information can make an activity more memorable and motivating. It is not important whether your learners' artwork is perfect or not. The pictures should only serve their purpose in the activity.

In the activities, the learners are focusing on the topic and communicating their ideas, rather than on the language, which helps motivate them to speak and at the same time not limit themselves in the choice of language they can use.

The teacher's role

You are an English teacher; you are not expected to know all about science, history, or biology. Your task is to help and assist the learners in language learning and at the same time stimulate their interest to find explanations or answers to questions rising from their work on cross-curricular topics. If you teach at a primary or secondary school, you can encourage the learners to discuss some of the issues with the teachers of other school subjects. You may find it useful to talk to your colleagues yourself and find out more about the topic you are going to teach. It will give you an idea of what work the learners have done with subject teachers. There are many units in the book that create a basis for cooperation between language and subject teachers. For example, in 'Stone Age' a history teacher can help you provide pictures or more information about prehistoric archaeological sites. In 'Leaves' you can cooperate with a biology teacher on making a herbarium. Invite a science or physics teacher for a few minutes to your class to answer the learners' questions about 'Experiments with a glass of water'. If you find cooperation with your colleagues enriching and motivating, you can try and prepare a new lesson plan together or teach a class together.

Conclusion

I hope you enjoy using the book and make the material your own. Adding and contributing your ideas to the lesson plans will help you to develop your teaching skills and help your learners to develop their language skills. I wish you luck and a lot of inspiration.

Activities

1 Coat of arms

TARGET LANGUAGE 'Personal qualities' vocabulary area
Animals and adjectives

CROSS-CURRICULAR LINKS Art, History, Biology

RESOURCES The board, a pencil and a sheet of paper for each learner,
coloured pencils for each pair of learners

PREPARATION Copy the coat of arms from stage 1 on the board.

TIME GUIDE 45–50 minutes

Lesson

1   Explain that the picture on the board is Christopher Columbus'
coat of arms. Let the class guess what the symbols mean. (Answer:
Columbus was made a knight and given a coat of arms for his
voyage in 1492 by King Fernando and Queen Isabel of Spain. The
castle (Castile) and the lion (Leon) are Spanish royal symbols. The
lion is also a symbol of courage and bravery. The islands in the sea
refer to Columbus' career as an explorer. The five anchors represent
the office of the Admiral of the Sea.)

2   Explain that coats of arms often depict animals. Write bee, lark, ox,
kitten, mouse, snail, and mule on the left-hand side of the board.
Get the learners to discuss what qualities are usually connected
with these animals and write their answers next to the animal.
Then write a list of colours on the right-hand side of the board and
ask the class what character types these colours might represent.
Write their answers next to the colour. For example:

lion – brave	white – optimistic
bee – busy	yellow – cheerful
lark – happy	orange – energetic
ox – strong	red – quick-tempered
kitten – playful	blue – creative
mouse – quiet	green – honest
snail – slow	brown – practical
mule – stubborn	black – lazy

3   Tell the learners that they are going to design their own coats of
arms. Ask the learners to decide which expressions and adjectives
from the list describe them and their personality best. Encourage
them to make those colours and images of animals part of their
design.

4   Give the learners sheets of paper and coloured pencils. Encourage them to make their design special and original. Ask them to follow the next five steps when drawing their coat of arms.

   a Draw an outline of your coat of arms.

   b Divide it into sections with lines. For example:

   c Choose a combination of colours from the list. Use them to colour in the sections.

   d Draw an animal or animals from the list.

   e Complete your coat of arms with another personal symbol that represents you, your interests, or hobbies. Do not write your name in the design.

5   Collect the coats of arms from the learners when they finish. Mix up the sheets and hand them out to different learners again. Make sure you do not give them back to their author.

6   Ask the learners to study the new coat of arms and decide what it tells them about its author. Tell them to think about whose coat of arms it can be.

7   Invite the learners to sit in a circle. Ask the learners to take turns and speak about the coat of arms they have been given. One learner at a time shows the design to the rest of the class, describes it in simple sentences, and guesses whose coat of arms it is. For example, 'The person is busy and he or she is optimistic, cheerful, and energetic. The person likes football and ice cream. … I think it's Pavel.' If the first guess is incorrect, invite other learners to join in and say who they think the author is and why.

8   When everyone has spoken, tell the learners to take their coats of arms back. Ask them to add their name and a motto (a short phrase that goes under the coat of arms) on the sheet, for example, 'Football-lover' or 'Busy bee', or a sentence about their likes, dislikes, or opinions, for example, 'Chocolate makes life easier'. Display their coats of arms with the mottos in the classroom.

2 Animals

TARGET LANGUAGE	'Animals' vocabulary area **Can, can't; have, don't have**
CROSS-CURRICULAR LINKS	Biology
RESOURCES	The board, a piece of paper and a pencil for each learner, blank stickers or small pieces of paper and pins
PREPARATION	Draw the pictures from stage 1 on the board.
TIME GUIDE	45 minutes

Lesson

1   Point to the board and explain to the learners that they can see parts of animals' bodies in the windows. Let them look at the pictures and guess which animals these are. Write the names of the animals on the board. (Answers: 1 – bird, 2 – monkey, 3 – snail, 4 – fish, 5 – bee or fly, 6 – crocodile, 7 – spider, 8 – elephant, 9 – frog, 10 – snake)

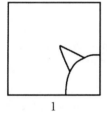 1   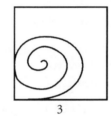 2   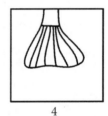 3    4   5

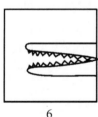 6   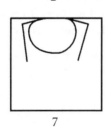 7   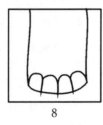 8   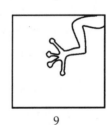 9    10

2   Use the pictures to elicit or teach the following expressions. Write them on the board.

Body parts: *wings, legs, feathers, scales, gills, a tail, a shell, a trunk, fur, a beak*

Actions: *swim, fly, jump, slither, crawl*

3   Give everyone a sheet of paper and a pencil. Ask them to write the names of the animals from the board on the sheet. Tell them to leave some space below each animal for notes. Ask the learners to decide which words from stage 2 go with each animal and list them, for example:

Bird	Crocodile	Monkey	Snail
wings	scales	legs	a shell
feathers	legs	a tail	slither
a tail	a tail	fur	
a beak	swim	jump	
fly			

Let the learners compare their lists in pairs.

4 Write these sentence frames on the board:

Do I have …?	Yes, you do. / No, you don't.
Can I …?	Yes, you can. / No, you can't.
Am I a/an …?	Yes, you are. / No, you're not.

5 Give one learner a blank sticker or a small piece of paper. Ask him or her to choose one of the animals from the board and write it on the sticker or paper. Do not look at what they write. Then ask the learner to stick or pin it to your clothes on the back. Let the learners see the word. Use the sentence frames from the board to ask them questions to learn which animal is on the sticker, for example, 'Do I have legs?', 'Can I fly?' Get the learners to answer your questions.

6 Divide the class into pairs. Give the learners stickers or pieces of paper. Ask them to choose three of the animals from the board and write them on the sticker. Tell them to stick or pin the words on each other's back. When all the learners have stickers on their backs, play the game as a whole-class activity. Tell the learners to ask each other questions to find out which three animals are written on their sticker – they can only ask one person one question. When a learner thinks they have the three answers, check the sticker for them.

7 Choose one animal and describe it using the structures 'I have …' and 'I can …', for example, 'I have a tail, scales, and gills, and I can swim. Who am I?' Get the class to say which animal it is.

8 Let the learners work in pairs. Ask them to choose animals, describe them to each other as you did in stage 7, and guess which animals they are.

3 Fractions

TARGET LANGUAGE   Numbers – fractions
Present perfect

CROSS-CURRICULAR LINKS   Maths

RESOURCES   The board, a pencil and a sheet of paper for each learner

PREPARATION   None

TIME GUIDE   45 minutes

Lesson

1   Draw five circles on the board. Invite five volunteers to come to the board and divide the circles into two, three, four, six, and eight equal parts:

2   Use the drawings to introduce some fractions, for example:

1/2	*a half*
1/3, 2/3	*a third, two thirds*
1/4, 3/4	*a quarter, three quarters*
1/6, 5/6	*a sixth, five sixths*
1/8	*an eighth*

3   Ask the learners to draw three circles in their notes and divide the first one into quarters, the second one into sixths, and the last one into eighths. Tell them it is Ann's birthday and the circles are birthday cakes cut into pieces. There is a vanilla cake, a strawberry cake, and a chocolate cake. Explain that members of her family have all eaten some cake. Ask the learners to listen and write the names of the family members in the section/s of the cake. Read the text:

Ann's father has eaten a quarter of the vanilla cake. Her mother loves chocolate so she has eaten an eighth of the chocolate cake. Ann's sister, who likes fruit, has eaten a sixth of the strawberry cake. Ann's brother loves cake – he's eaten a quarter of the chocolate cake and a sixth of the strawberry cake. Then grandfather has eaten a quarter of the vanilla cake and grandmother an eighth of the chocolate cake. Ann's uncle has eaten an eighth of the chocolate cake and a sixth of the strawberry one. Her aunt has only eaten an eighth of the chocolate cake.

Ask the learners to use their notes and calculate how many sections of each cake are left.

vanilla   strawberry   chocolate

(Answers: 2/4 or 1/2 of the vanilla cake, 3/6 or 1/2 of the strawberry cake and 2/8, or 1/4 of the chocolate cake.)

4 Draw the following items on the board:

mushroom pizza   ham and cheese pizza   apple   watermelon

5 Ask the learners to draw the same pictures on their paper. Divide the class into pairs. Tell the pairs that this is a picture of a meal they are going to share. Ask everyone to decide how much he or she would like to eat from the meal and mark it in his or her drawing.

6 Write *I'd like to have …* on the board and ask the learners to tell each other about their choice. They may have to compromise if both of them want to eat the same food. Encourage them to use fractions, for example, 'I'd like to have a quarter of the mushroom pizza, a third of the ham and cheese pizza, and a quarter of the watermelon.' Tell them to mark their partner's choice in their picture, too. Then invite each of them to calculate from the picture how much food is left. Ask them to write the answer down and compare the result with their partner.

7 Tell the class to make new pairs and draw the items from stage 5 again. Invite the learners to tell each other about how much their partner and they have eaten from the first meal and mark the amounts in their charts. For example, 'Denisa has eaten a quarter of the mushroom pizza and an eighth of the watermelon. I have eaten a third of the ham and cheese pizza, a quarter of the mushroom pizza, and two halves of the apple / the whole apple.' Ask them to calculate how much food is left from their partner's meal, write the answer down, and compare it with their partner's calculation.

4 Drawing a song

TARGET LANGUAGE	Song lyrics
CROSS-CURRICULAR LINKS	Art, Music
RESOURCES	A sheet of paper for each learner, (coloured) pencils, lyrics of a song written on the board or on a poster
PREPARATION	Make the poster or write the lyrics on the board.
TIME GUIDE	45 minutes

Lesson

1 Prepare a poster with the song's lyrics or write the lyrics on the board before the lesson. This unit works with the lyrics of *Cockles and Mussels* as an example. You can, however, adapt the idea to any song you wish to teach.

2 Tell the learners they are going to draw pictures based on a song. Put up the poster or use the lyrics on the board. Ask the learners to listen to the song and watch the lyrics. Sing the song for the class. If you cannot sing, you can read the lyrics as a poem. Get the learners to ask about the words they do not understand and explain their meaning. Then read the whole text together.

3 Give each learner a sheet of paper. Divide the song into sections. In most songs you can use lines. For example, in *Cockles and Mussels*, each line can be used as an independent image:

> *In Dublin's fair city, where the girls are so pretty*
> *I first set my eyes on sweet Molly Malone*
> *As she wheeled her wheel-barrow*
> *Through streets broad and narrow*
> *Crying cockles and mussels, alive, alive-O!*

Assign each line to a different learner. If you have fewer lines than learners, let them work in pairs. If you have more lines than learners, let some learners work on two images. In this case make sure that they have two sheets of paper. Tell the learners to write their lines on the paper.

4 Ask the learners to turn the sheets on the other side. Encourage them to draw a picture representing what their line is about. Tell them not to worry at all about how good their drawing is going to be.

5 Borrow a drawing from one learner. Show it to the class and ask them which line they think the picture represents. Point at the lyrics on the poster or the board and invite the learners to use them. Do not reject any suggestions. After they have guessed, turn the picture over and read which line it is.

6 Ask the learners to walk around and show their pictures to each other, guessing which lines they have drawn. They can use the lyrics on the board or poster as reference.

7 Invite everyone to sit in their seats again and join you in reading the lyrics of the song from the poster or board. Pause after each line. The learner with the drawing representing the line you have just read stands up and hands you the drawing. Pile the pictures one after another in the order they occur in the song.

8 Take the pictures you have piled up and show them to the learners one after another. Get them to say the lines the pictures represent.

9 Teach the tune and sing the whole song together with the help of the pictures. If the learners do not remember all the lines, the text on the poster or the board can help them.

COCKLES AND MUSSELS *(Traditional Irish song)*

In Dublin's fair city, where the girls are so pretty
I first set my eyes on sweet Molly Malone
As she wheeled her wheel-barrow
Through streets broad and narrow
Crying cockles and mussels, alive, alive-O!

Chorus: Alive, alive-O! alive, alive-O!

Crying cockles and mussels, alive, alive-O!
She was a fish-monger, but sure 'twas no wonder
For so were her father and mother before
And they each wheeled their barrow
Through streets broad and narrow
Crying cockles and mussels, alive, alive-O!

Chorus: Alive, alive-O! …

She died of a fever, and no one could save her
And that was the end of sweet Molly Malone
But her ghost wheels her barrow
Through streets broad and narrow
Crying cockles and mussels, alive, alive-O!

Chorus: Alive, alive-O! …

5 Plants

TARGET LANGUAGE	'Plants' vocabulary area
	Present simple
	Question forms – **Does it …?, Do you …?, Has it got …?**
CROSS-CURRICULAR LINKS	Biology
RESOURCES	The board, a sheet of paper and a pencil for each learner
PREPARATION	Draw the picture from stage 1 on the blackboard.
TIME GUIDE	45 minutes

Lesson

1 Point to the drawing on the board and tell the learners that you grow plants at home: a *tulip*, a *bean*, a *cactus*, some *basil*, and some *garlic*. Explain that you grow the plants in pots from *seeds* and *bulbs*, or one part of a bulb called a *clove*. Only the cactus is from the flower shop. Show where the plants have *leaves*, *stems*, and *flowers*. Point out that the bean has *pods* with seeds and the cactus a stem with *spines*.

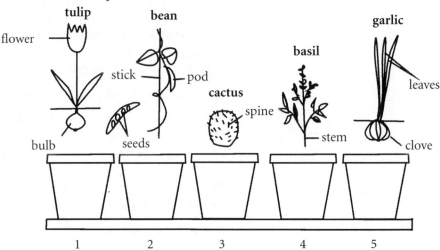

2 Give everyone a sheet of paper and a pencil. Ask them to write the numbers 1 to 5 on the sheet. Tell the learners that you are going to describe which plant you grow in each flowerpot. Ask them to listen and write the letters next to the numbers. Describe the plants in simple sentences, for example:

a The plant grows very quickly. It has a stick in the pot to climb on. It has red flowers and then green pods. I sometimes use the seeds from the pods in the kitchen.

b I grow the plant from a clove. The leaves are long and narrow. I cut the leaves and use them on sandwiches. They taste milder than the cloves. I also use the cloves for cooking.

10

c The plant has shiny green leaves. The leaves have a very pleasant and sweet taste. I add them to salads and other dishes. I water the plant very often. It likes sunlight.

d It's a desert plant. It needs very little water, especially in the winter. It likes a lot of sunlight. It has no leaves, but a thick stem with spines.

e It's a spring plant. It has a tall stem and a large bright flower shaped like a cup. I grow the plant from a bulb. The plant doesn't like it when it is too hot.

(Answers: a – bean, b – garlic, c – basil, d – cactus, e – tulip)

3 Check the answers with the class.

4 Tell the learners that you are going to describe the plants again. This time ask them to listen and write simple notes – the main nouns, verbs, and adjectives – about each plant. For example:

Cactus: desert plant, needs little water, a lot of sunlight, no leaves, stem with spines.

Pause between sentences to give the learners time to think and write.

5 Ask the learners to dictate you their notes for each plant and write them on the board. Then ask the class to fill out the notes to make full sentences.

6 Divide the learners into pairs. Explain that each person should choose a plant in secret and they have to ask five questions to learn which plant their partner has chosen. The partner can only answer 'Yes' or 'No'. Tell them to count a point for each 'Yes' they get from their partner. The points only count when they guess the plant. Ask them to compare who has got more points in the end. For example:

LEARNER 1 *Has the plant got pods?*
LEARNER 2 *No.*
LEARNER 1 *Do you use it for cooking?*
LEARNER 2 *Yes.*
LEARNER 1 *Does it grow from a clove?*
LEARNER 2 *No.*
LEARNER 1 *Has the plant got shiny leaves?*
LEARNER 2 *Yes.*
LEARNER 1 *Do you add the leaves to salads?*
LEARNER 2 *Yes.*
LEARNER 1 *It's basil.*

(Three points)

6 Experiments with a glass of water

TARGET LANGUAGE   First conditional

CROSS-CURRICULAR LINKS   Science

RESOURCES   The board, a sheet of paper and pen (or pencil) for each learner, a round glass or jar with water, a paper clip, a needle, a fork, two coins of the same size, a pencil, and a piece of modelling clay (or aluminium foil).

PREPARATION   Write the questions from stage 2 on the board. Try the experiments before the lesson.

TIME GUIDE   45 minutes

Lesson

1 Tell the learners you are going to do some experiments with water. Show them all the materials you are going to use (see 'Resources' above) and check the class know what they are called.

2 Read through the questions you have written on the board. Explain any words the learners do not understand.

   a What will happen if you put a paper clip in a glass of water? Will it sink or float?

   b What will happen if you put a needle in a glass of water? Will it sink or float?

   c What will happen if you put a coin in a glass of water? Will the coin look larger or smaller?

   d What will happen if you put a pencil in a glass of water? Will the pencil look larger, smaller, or broken?

   e What will happen if you put a piece of modelling clay in a glass of water? Will it sink or float?

3 Divide the class into two groups. Ask one group to move to the back of the classroom. Tell them to practise reading out the questions and in small groups discuss what they think will happen in the experiments.

4 Prepare all the materials you need for the experiments on the desk at the front. Ask the other group to join you and stand around the desk.

5 Carry out the experiments. Introduce each experiment with the question from the board. Ask the learners not to answer the questions aloud yet. Make sure everyone in the group can see the result.

   a *Use a round glass/jar with water. Place the paper clip on the fork. Slowly lower the fork and gently put the paper clip on the surface of the water. Take the fork away. If you are slow and careful, the paper clip will float.*

a   b   c   d   e

b *Place the needle on the fork. Lower the fork as you did in the first experiment and make the needle float. If you drop it quickly, it will sink.*

c *Drop one coin in the water. Place the other one next to the glass. Look at the coin in the water from the side. It will look larger.*

d *Put the pencil in the glass of water. Make sure a part of it is in the air. Look at the pencil from the side. It looks broken. The part in the water also looks a little larger.*

e *Roll a piece of modelling clay/aluminium foil into a ball. Drop it in the water. It will sink. Remove it from the glass. Now shape the piece of clay/foil into a boat. Place it on the water surface. It should float.*

6   Pair up the learners from the two groups. Let the learners who have not seen the experiments interview the learners who have. Invite them to use the questions from the board.

7   Do the experiments with the whole class again. This time you can invite a learner to the desk to carry them out. Get the other learners to describe each experiment, for example:

a/b If you drop the paper clip/needle slowly with a fork, the paper clip/needle will float. If you drop it quickly, it will sink.

c   If you look at the coin in the water from the side, it will look larger.

d   If you look at the pencil in the water from the side, it will look broken.

e   If you roll the clay into a ball, it will sink. But if you shape it into a boat, it will float.

8   Write the following sentence on the board: *If you drop a needle in a glass of water slowly, it will float.* Give each learner a sheet of paper. Ask them to write five similar sentences about the experiments. Encourage them to use the phrase: 'If you …, it will …'. Walk around as they are writing and offer help or feedback.

7 Gold Rush routes

TARGET LANGUAGE	'Travelling and transportation' vocabulary area Past simple
CROSS-CURRICULAR LINKS	Geography, History
RESOURCES	The board, a sheet of paper and a pencil for each learner
PREPARATION	Draw the map from stage 1 on the board.
TIME GUIDE	45 minutes

Lesson

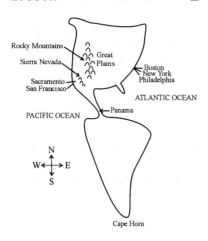

1 Ask the learners to copy the map. Explain that in 1849 gold was discovered near Sacramento in California. Thousands of people from the eastern United States headed there to look for gold and become rich. Tell the learners you are going to describe three popular routes the people from the Atlantic coast took to get to California. Ask them to listen and mark the routes in pencil on their maps. Repeat the descriptions as many times as necessary.

Route 1: Some gold-seekers reached California by sea. They took a ship from one of the Atlantic ports (New York, Boston, or Philadelphia) and sailed around Cape Horn, the southern tip of South America, and then went up the Pacific coast to San Francisco.

Route 2: Some travellers took a short cut. They boarded a ship to take them from one of the Atlantic ports to Panama in Central America. They walked across the land to find another ship on the west coast. Another ship carried them north to San Francisco.

Route 3: Another way to California was by land. The gold-seekers travelling overland first passed the Great Plains. Then they crossed the mountains in the west, such as the Rocky Mountains or the Sierra Nevada, to reach Sacramento in California.

2 Ask the learners to compare their maps in pairs. Then invite three volunteers to mark the three routes on the board.

3 Draw this chart on the board. Ask the learners to copy it.

	Around South America	Across Panama	Overland
Transportation			
Time			
Cost			
Possible danger			

4 Get the learners to predict how much time and money a traveller needed to complete the journey from the Atlantic coast to California at that time and what possible danger he or she faced on each route. Discuss the means of transportation the traveller could take on each route.

5 Read the following information about the routes. Ask the learners to listen and write simple notes about each route in the chart. Read out the text a few times, pausing between sentences to give the learners time to think and write.

Route 1: Sailing by ship around South America usually took at least 6 months. The passengers paid between $150 and $1,200 for a ticket. The ships were often overcrowded. At Cape Horn the travellers faced violent storms and many of them got seasick. Some ships were overturned and many passengers drowned.

Route 2: The gold-seekers who took a short cut across Panama had to change ships. In 1849 there was no Panama Canal. The travellers walked across the land and waited for another ship on the other side. Sometimes waiting for a ship on the west coast took weeks. The ticket cost around $500. It was possible to reach California in about four months. Crossing Panama meant walking along swamps and muddy trails. Some gold-seekers caught malaria there and died.

Route 3: People heading for California overland went by horse, wagon, mule, or just on foot. It took 5–6 months to reach California in this way. A family of four usually paid between $600 and $700 for the trip. The overland journey had its dangers, too. People often ran out of food and had trouble finding clean water or grass for their animals. Many people became ill and died from drinking dirty water.

6 Check the learners' notes. Explain any expressions the learners are not familiar with.

7 Divide the class into groups of four. Ask them to imagine they are four friends who want to travel to California together to look for gold. Tell them to discuss the routes, consider their advantages and disadvantages, and then agree on one they are going to take.

8 Ask the groups about their decision. Which route have they chosen? Why?

8 Multiplying and dividing

TARGET LANGUAGE
Numbers and calculations using **multiplied by, times, equals, divided by**
There is/are, how many, each
Prepositions of place

CROSS-CURRICULAR LINKS
Maths

RESOURCES
The board, a sheet of paper and a pencil for each learner

PREPARATION
Prepare stories to tell. See stage 4.

TIME GUIDE
45 minutes

Lesson

1 Tell the learners that you are going to tell a simple story which you just want them to listen to. For example:

> In the street where I live there are two hotels. In each hotel there are five floors. On each floor there are ten rooms. In each room there is a bathroom. In each bathroom there are two bars of soap. Then one day a thief steals half the soap bars. How many bars of soap are left in the hotel rooms?

2 Give each learner a sheet of paper and a pencil to make notes. Repeat the story. This time pause between the sentences to give the learners time to think and count. Get the learners to ask you questions if they missed some numbers, for example, 'How many rooms are there?' Check their answers.

3 Go through the story again and write a simple equation on the board to show how the problem can be solved. (Answer: 2 x 5 x 10 x 1 x 2 = 200; 200 ÷ 2 = 100.) Get the learners to help you explain the procedure. For example:

TEACHER   *There are two hotels in the town. How many floors are there in each hotel?*
LEARNERS   *Five.*
TEACHER   *Yes, there are five floors in each hotel. Two times five, how much is that?*
LEARNERS   *Ten.*
TEACHER   *That's right. There are ten floors altogether. How many rooms are there on each floor?*
LEARNERS   *Ten.*
TEACHER   *Yes, there are ten rooms on each floor. Ten times ten is …*
LEARNERS   *A hundred.*
TEACHER   *Good. There are a hundred rooms altogether. Now, how many bathrooms are there in both the hotels?*
LEARNERS   *A hundred.*
TEACHER   *Yes, a hundred. Each room has got one bathroom. In*

each bathroom there are two bars of soap. A hundred multiplied by two equals …

LEARNERS *Two hundred.*

TEACHER *Good. Two hundred soap bars in both the hotels. And then a thief steals half of them. Two hundred divided by two makes …*

LEARNERS *One hundred.*

4 Tell the learners more stories. Encourage them to ask questions again if they miss any numbers. For example:

a There are two floors in the school. On each floor there are five classrooms. In each classroom there are three rows. In each row there are four desks. At each desk there are two chairs. How many chairs are there in the school? (Answer: 2 x 5 x 3 x 4 x 2 = 240 chairs.)

b In the hospital close to where I live there are four floors. On each floor there are five rooms. In each room there are two patients. Each patient has got two pillows. There is an extra pillow in each room. How many pillows are there in the hospital altogether? (Answer: 4 x 5 x 2 = 40 x 2 + 40 = 120 pillows.)

c There are three flower shops. In each flower shop there are ten flowerpots. In each flowerpot there are eight tulips. Half of the tulips are yellow. How many yellow tulips are there in the flower shops? (Answer: 3 x 10 x 8 = 240 tulips, 240 ÷ 2 = 120 yellow tulips.)

d A zoo buys two hundred and ten carrots for rabbits every week. There are two rabbit hutches in the zoo. In each rabbit hutch there are five rabbits. How many carrots can each rabbit eat every day? (Answer: 210 carrots, 10 rabbits, 7 days; 210 ÷ 7 = 30 carrots a day; 30 ÷ 10 = 3 carrots for each rabbit a day.)

Check the learners' answers. Invite them to explain in simple language how they arrived at the results.

5 Write the following sentence patterns on the board:

There is/are …
In/on/at each … there are …
Each … has got …
How many … are there …?

6 Ask the learners to use the sentence frames and write a similar story with numbers that are easy to multiply or divide. When they have finished, ask them to tell the story to at least two other learners and let them calculate the result. In the end invite a few learners to share their stories with the whole class.

9 Leaves

TARGET LANGUAGE	Question forms Describing shapes, sizes, and surfaces
CROSS-CURRICULAR LINKS	Biology, Art
RESOURCES	The board, leaves, a sheet of paper for each learner, pencils Paper leaves: pieces of paper of different colours, thickness, and texture, scissors
PREPARATION	Pick some real leaves or make paper ones. Write the questions from stage 2 on the board.
TIME GUIDE	45 minutes

Lesson

1 Ask the learners to bring real leaves into class. Encourage them to choose leaves they know and which have interesting shapes, sizes, colours, or textures. Pick some leaves yourself and bring them to the lesson. If you do not want to or cannot work with real leaves, make paper ones. Prepare pieces of paper of different colours, thickness, and textures. You can use old paper boxes, wrapping paper, paper napkins, or pages from newspapers or magazines. Copy the shapes of leaves in different sizes from the picture below on the paper and cut them out with scissors.

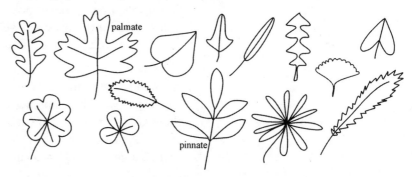

2 Hold a leaf up so that the class can see. Ask questions about the leaf using the examples below. Explain the words the learners do not know. Show other leaves, use gestures, or draw to teach new expressions.

Size	*Is the leaf*	*large, medium-sized, or small?*
Shape	*Is it*	*a single or compound leaf?* *round, oval, or heart-shaped?* *long, narrow, or pointed?* *pinnate (the leaf has small separate leaves, for example, an ash)?* *palmate (there is just one big leaf, for example, a maple)?*

Texture	Is it	rough or smooth?
		thick or thin?
		hairy or shiny?
	Has it got	big or small veins?
Edges	Has it got	smooth, toothed, or rounded edges?
Colour	Is it	light/dark green, red, brown, or yellow?

Get the learners to answer your questions. Underline or tick the words they used to describe the leaf. If you work with paper leaves, leave out the words that are not relevant. You may want to point out the irregular plural of the word leaf – 'leaves'. Practise saying /θ/ in *th*ick, *th*in and too*th*. Show the class how to make the sound by putting your tongue between your teeth and breathing out.

3 Invite the learners to prepare their leaves. Ask them to write *Size*, *Shape*, *Texture*, *Edges*, and *Colour* on a sheet of paper. Tell them to work on their own, read through the questions on the board, and make notes about their leaf.

4 Ask the learners to show each other their leaves. Encourage them to ask the questions from the board to at least three other learners and compare their answers with the notes.

5 Divide the class into groups of four to play a simple game. Ask them to sit around one desk and lay a selection of different leaves out on it. One learner in each group chooses one of the leaves in his or her head. The others ask him or her Yes/No questions to learn which one it is. The learners take turns choosing the leaves.

Follow-up
Make a collection of dry leaves (herbarium) with the learners. Teach the learners to press the leaves between two sheets of paper inside heavy books. The leaves should be pressed for about two weeks and then glued on sheets of paper. Ask the learners to write a description for each leaf including the information about its size, shape, texture, edges, and colour, and a sentence about when and where the leaf was picked.

Variation
Use rubbings instead of pressed leaves. Place a fresh leaf under a sheet of paper; the bumpy side (the side with the raised veins) faces up. Gently rub a pencil or crayon over the paper where the leaf is.

10 Health

TARGET LANGUAGE	'Health' vocabulary area **Should** for giving advice Present perfect
CROSS-CURRICULAR LINKS	Biology, Drama
RESOURCES	The board
PREPARATION	Copy this text and the pictures on the board:

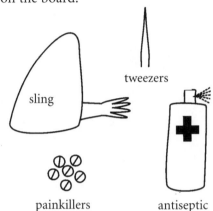

bandage

thermometer

nasal drops

plaster

sling

tweezers

painkillers

antiseptic

Take your temperature.
Put a plaster on.
Have it X-rayed.
Drink plenty of fluids.
Remove it with tweezers.
Put it in a sling.
Use some nasal drops.
Wrap a bandage around it.
Put a plastic bag with ice on it.
Put some antiseptic on.
See a doctor.
Take a painkiller.

TIME GUIDE	45 minutes

Lesson

1   Tell the learners you are sick or have had an accident. Use the following sentences to tell them what is wrong with you. Get them to use the language from the board to give you advice. Help with vocabulary if necessary.

I think I've broken my arm.
Oh, I've cut my finger.
I've got a terrible headache. It's probably flu.
I've got a splinter.
I've got a cold. My nose is congested. I can't breathe.
I think I've sprained my ankle.

2   Divide the class into two groups, A and B. Tell the learners they are going to walk around the classroom and talk to each other in open pairs. The As pretend they are sick or injured. The Bs give the As advice on what they should do.

LEARNER 1   *I've got a terrible cold. My nose is blocked. What should I do?*
LEARNER 2   *I think you should use some nasal drops.*

3 The learners continue walking round the classroom and talking in pairs. This time ask the As to describe the advice they got for their injuries or symptoms to the Bs. The Bs guess what medical problems the As have. For example:

LEARNER 1 *I should see a doctor and have it X-rayed. Maybe, I should put it in a sling.*

LEARNER 2 *I think you've broken your arm.*

4 Divide the class into groups of four. Ask the learners to imagine that they are actors working on a TV sketch. Two of them act out a dialogue, without speaking, about being unwell and giving advice. The other two actors, chosen by the director of the programme, do the speaking. Let them decide who wants to act and who wants to do the speaking. If there is not an equal number of male/female learners in the group, a male voice can be used for a female actor and vice versa. The effect of such an arrangement is usually comical. Encourage the pair doing the acting to move their lips and use a lot of gestures, while the other pair, doing the speaking, should try to match the dialogue with the action. Give the groups a few minutes to practise their sketches.

5 Use the space in front of the board as a stage. Reserve a couple of seats at the front for the learners who do the speaking. Make sure they can see the actors from the seats. Invite the groups, one after another, to come to the stage and perform their sketches.

11 Moving pictures

TARGET LANGUAGE   Present simple
Present continuous

CROSS-CURRICULAR LINKS   Art

RESOURCES   Story on the scroll: the board, three pencils and two sheets of paper for each learner; scissors, sellotape, glue. Animation: a pencil and 2 strips of paper for each learner, each strip about 20 x 7cm; cut 4 strips from an A4 sheet.

PREPARATION   Story on a scroll: Write the questions from stage 1 on the board. Animation: Prepare two strips of paper with pictures to demonstrate the activity in Animation, stage 1.

 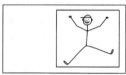

TIME GUIDE   Story on the scroll: 45–60 minutes
Animation: 20–30 minutes

Lesson

Story on a scroll

1 Tell the learners that they are going to write a simple story and then make it into a cartoon scroll with pictures. Use the questions on the board as a guideline for writing the story. Explain that questions 5–7 relate to past events and that they can use the Present simple tense to tell a story that happened in the past. Follow the questions and tell the learners a story as an example.

1 Who is the character? What is his/her name?
2 Where does he/she live?
3 What does he/she like?
4 What does he/she dislike?
5 What happens one day? Where does the character go?
6 What does he/she see there?
7 What does he/she do?

For example: 1 Punt'a is our dog. 2 He lives with us in the house. 3 He likes playing with a ball. 4 He does not like our neighbour's cat Minda. 5 One day I go for a walk with him. 6 Suddenly, he sees Minda. 7 He starts chasing her.

2 Give everyone a sheet of paper and a pencil. Encourage them to follow the questions on the board and write a story about a character of their choice. Walk around the classroom as they are writing and offer help.

3 When the learners have finished, hand out another sheet of paper and two more pencils. Ask the learners to follow your instructions:

Hold the paper horizontally, fold it, and then cut into two pieces with the scissors. Stick the pieces together with glue or sellotape to make a scroll. Draw seven frames on the scroll for the cartoon (see Picture A). Use each frame to tell one part of the story. Draw the pictures for the story in the frames. Attach a pencil to each side of the scroll with sellotape. Roll up the scroll on the pencils to show the first frame of the cartoon (see Picture B). Hold on the pencils and roll them to move the frames.

Picture A   Picture B

4 Invite the learners to manipulate their scrolls by rolling the pencils. Ask them to show their cartoon frame by frame and tell their story to other learners.

Animation

1 Invite the learners to come to the front of the classroom and watch. Take one of the strips and roll it up on a pencil (see Picture A). Stop when you have rolled up more than a half of it and cannot see the picture any more (see Picture B).

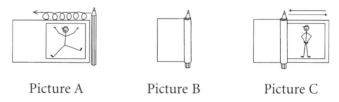

Picture A   Picture B   Picture C

2 Take the strip with the pencil and place it on the other one, left corners matching. Put your finger in the upper left corner to make both the strips stay together. Next, move the pencil back and forth quickly, showing and hiding the picture in the rolled-up strip again and again (see Picture C). When you watch the frames, the image in them will appear to be moving. Get the learners to describe what they see – 'The man is jumping.'

3 Give each learner two strips of paper and a pencil. Tell them to imagine two different stages of the same action they can draw and describe in English. Repeat the directions for them after they finish drawing pictures on their own strips. Invite them to show their moving images to other learners in the class and let the others describe what they can see using the Present continuous.

12 Weather

TARGET LANGUAGE	'Weather' vocabulary area Adverbs of frequency – **usually, often, sometimes, rarely** Present continuous and Present simple
CROSS-CURRICULAR LINKS	Geography, Art
RESOURCES	The board, a sheet of paper and a pencil for each learner
PREPARATION	Draw the pictures from stage 1 without the words, and the text from stage 4 on the board.
TIME GUIDE	45 minutes

Lesson

1 Ask the learners to give you the adjectives to fit the weather symbols and write the answers on the board.

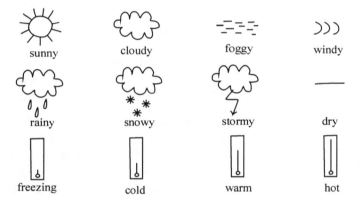

Then ask what the nouns and verbs are:

Adjectives	sunny	cloudy	foggy	windy	rainy	snowy	stormy	dry
Nouns	sun	cloud	fog	wind	rain	snow	storm	–
Verbs	shine	–	–	blow	rain	snow	–	–

2 Draw the weather symbols from stage 1 in the window to indicate different kinds of weather. Use the chalk/marker and the sponge to add and wipe the symbols. For example:

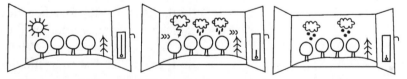

Get the learners to describe the changes of the weather in the window in as much detail as they can. For example: 'It's dry, sunny, and hot', 'It's windy and stormy', 'It's raining', 'It's rather cold', 'It's freezing', 'It's snowing', etc.

3 Ask the learners to check what the weather is like outside and describe it.

4 Work with the text you wrote on the board before the lesson.

Spring weather is usually ⬜ . It often ☁ and it's ☁ , but there are ☀ days, too. Sometimes the weather can be dangerous and there are ☁ . It rarely ☁ in the spring, but it can be))) and ⬜ .

5 Ask the learners to help you decode the text. Read out the sentences, but pause before the pictures and let the learners fill the missing words: *warm, rains, cloudy, sunny, storms, snows, windy, cold.*

6 Underline *usually, often, sometimes,* and *rarely* in the text on the board. Explain that the words suggest how often things happen. In the text the adverbs of frequency occur arranged in a scale (*usually – often – sometimes – rarely*) from the most frequent to the least frequent. Use the examples from the text to point out where in the sentence we place such adverbs (after *is/are*, before verbs like *rain/snow*; *sometimes* can stand at the beginning of the sentence, too).

7 Give each learner a sheet of paper and a pencil. Tell them to fold the paper and tear it in half. Ask them to work on their own and choose one season in the year: summer, autumn, or winter. Ask them to think about the weather typical of the season and write a few sentences about it. Tell them not to mention in the text which season it is.

8 When the learners finish writing, invite them to substitute some expressions in their sentences with pictures or symbols. They can use the pictures from the board (stage 1) and also invent their own symbols for other expressions. Ask them to write the encoded text on the second piece of paper.

9 Divide the class into pairs. Invite them to exchange their encoded texts, read them out to their partner, and guess which season is described. Ask them to show each other the original text when they finish.

13 Measurements

TARGET LANGUAGE   'Measurements' vocabulary area
Numbers

CROSS-CURRICULAR LINKS   Maths, Biology, History

RESOURCES   The board, a sheet of paper, a pencil and a ruler for each learner

PREPARATION   Draw the picture from stage 1 on the board.

TIME GUIDE   45 minutes

Lesson

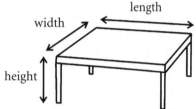

1   Use the picture or a piece of real furniture to show the learners the three dimensions:

Noun	Adjective	Question
height	high	How high …?
length	long	How long …?
width	wide	How wide …?

Explain that when we ask about the dimensions we can use the adjectives 'high', 'long', and 'wide', for example, 'How long is the desk?', 'How wide is the chair?', 'How high is the board?'.

2   Make sure each learner has a sheet of paper, a pencil, and a ruler. Ask the learners to use their rulers and measure in centimetres how high their chair is from the top of the back to the bottom of the legs. Tell them to ask two other learners about their measurements and compare the results, using the question, 'How high is your chair?'. Check with the class whether all the chairs in the classroom are the same height.

3   Tell the learners about measures people in ancient Egypt used. Write the names of the measures on the board. Demonstrate the measures as you are describing them:

1 cubit   the distance from your elbow to the tip of your middle finger
1 palm   the distance across your palm
1 digit   the width of your middle finger

4   Divide the class into groups of four. Ask each group to choose one chair. Tell all the members in the group to measure the height of the chair in cubits, palms, and digits on their own, for example, 'The chair is 1 cubit, 4 palms, and 3 digits high.' Ask the learners to compare their measurements with other learners in the group. Are they different? Why or why not? Their measurements will most probably be slightly different because their arms and hands are not of the same length and width.

5 Ask the learners to measure the length of their arm from their elbow to the tip of the middle finger and the width of their palm in centimetres. Tell them to ask each other about their results, using 'How long is your arm?' and 'How wide is your palm?'. Ask them if they can find someone else in class who has the same measurements.

6 Explain 'inch' and 'foot':

1 inch = about 2.5 centimetres (cm) or 2.54cm exactly.
1 foot = 12 inches (in)
1 foot = about 30cm or 30.48cm exactly.

Ask the learners to measure the length of their shoe with the ruler. Is their foot longer or shorter than 30cm? Get the learners to compare their measurements using 'How long is your foot?'. Ask them to find the person with the measurement closest to one foot.

7 Draw the following table on the board:

Dimension	Measurement
length	cm
	ft/in
width	cm
	ft/in
height	cm
	ft/in

Ask the learners to draw two tables like this on their sheets. Divide the class into pairs. Ask the pairs to choose one object in the classroom to measure. One learner in each pair measures it in centimetres, the other one in feet and inches. Tell the pairs to write the results of their measurements in the first chart on the sheets.

8 Write the following substitution table on the board:

How	long	is it in	centimetres?	It's ... centimetres	long.
	wide		feet and inches?	It's ... foot/feet ... inches	wide.
	high				high.

9 Ask each pair to exchange their measurements with another pair. Tell the learners to ask each other questions to learn about the measurements the other pair carried out and write them down in the second chart. Then ask the learners to go and try to find the object the measurements refer to.

14 The Stone Age

TARGET LANGUAGE	Past simple and Present simple 'Everyday life' vocabulary area
CROSS-CURRICULAR LINKS	History
RESOURCES	The board, a sheet of paper and a pencil for each learner; a stone and a piece of chalk
PREPARATION	Draw the picture from stage 1 on the stone. Draw an empty chart for stage 2 on the board.
TIME GUIDE	45–50 minutes

Lesson

1 Show the drawing on the stone to the learners. Ask them to guess which historical period you are going to talk about. Elicit what the learners know and can say about the Stone Age. Help them using the background information.

Background information

The Stone Age is the first period in human history. The Stone Age started about 2.5 million years ago. There are no written records from that time. Archaeologists have found:

— *cave paintings, for example, the Lascaux Cave in France, the Altamira Cave in Spain*
— *sculptures or carvings, for example, the Venus figure in Dolní Věstonice in the Czech Republic*
— *rock carvings, for example, in Alta, Norway*
— *objects and structures Stone Age people created, for example, tools from Olduvai Gorge in Tanzania, the standing stones in Stonehenge, England*
— *bones, for example in Lake Mungo, Australia.*

Archaeologists study the findings to learn how Stone Age people lived.

2 Elicit some ideas about how Stone Age people lived from the learners and fill in the chart.

	How did Stone Age people live?	How do you live today?
Home	They lived in caves or built their homes from stone, wood, and animal skins or bones.	
	They slept on the floor.	
	They used fire to heat their homes.	
Household jobs	They cleaned the animal skins and made tools from flint stone.	
Food	They hunted animals with bows and arrows, fished with harpoons in the river, or collected food.	
	They stored food in baskets or clay pots.	
Clothes	They made their clothes of animal fur or skin.	
Transportation	They walked everywhere.	
Art	They painted pictures on the walls in caves.	

3 Work with the text on the board. Get the learners to compare their life with the one Stone Age people lived. Ask questions to help the learners compare, for example, 'Where do you live?', 'Do you make your own clothes?', 'Where do you buy your food?', 'Where do you store food at home?', 'What household jobs do you do?', 'Do you walk to school?', etc. Help with vocabulary, if necessary. Write their suggestions on the board. For example:

We live in flats and houses built of brick, metal, cement, and glass.
We sleep in beds with pillows and blankets.
We use central heating to heat our homes.
We help with washing the dishes, vacuuming the carpet, and putting the rubbish out.
We buy our food in shops and supermarkets.
We store food in fridges and kitchen cupboards.
We buy our clothes in shops and department stores.
We ride bicycles, drive cars, travel by bus, train, or plane.
We paint, draw, and write on paper, and also on the computer.

4 Divide the class into two groups, a Stone Age team and a 21st century team. Ask the learners to imagine that they live in two different historical periods. Invite the 21st century team to interview the Stone Age team about how they live. Encourage them to use the language from the board or their own ideas and imagination to ask and answer questions. Next, ask the Stone Age team to interview the 21st century people.

15 Sight

TARGET LANGUAGE   Giving instructions
                     Present perfect

CROSS-CURRICULAR LINKS   Biology, Science

RESOURCES   The board, sheets of paper for making posters, metal spoons,
                     mirrors, a sheet of paper and a pencil for each learner

PREPARATION   Copy the texts and pictures from stage 2 on the posters.

TIME GUIDE   45 minutes

Lesson

1 Copy the following images on the board.

Ƨ⚯ЯAWꟼƆAꓭ   ∩ЬƧIDE DOMИ

Ask the learners what is wrong with them. (Answer: The first one is written backwards and the second one upside down.) Can the learners read them? Hold a mirror to the left or to the right of the first word. Ask a learner to come closer and tell the others how he or she sees the image in the mirror. The mirror image reflects the word the way we usually write it (*BACKWARDS*). Next, hold the mirror above the second word. Again, the reflection shows the word the way it should be written (*UPSIDE DOWN*).

2 Divide the class into four groups, A, B, C, and D. If you teach a big class, make more groups of the same letter. Tell the learners that each group is going to do a different experiment. Give each group one poster with the instructions how to carry it out. Hand out metal spoons to the learners in the group B and mirrors to the group D.

A
Close your left eye.
Put up your finger and line it up with a distant object.
Next, without moving the finger, close your right eye and open the left one.
What has happened to the finger?

B
Hold a spoon.
Look at the back of the spoon (the convex side).
Can you see your reflection?
Now, turn it round and look at the other side of the spoon (the concave side).
What has happened to your reflection?

concave

convex

C
Do the experiment in pairs.
Place your hands over your eyes
as if you were looking at
something in the bright sunlight.
Ask your partner to watch your
pupils.
Next, quickly remove the hands.
What has happened to the pupils?

D
Hold a mirror.
Touch your right ear.
Look at yourself in the mirror.
Which ear is the mirror image
touching?
Write your name on a piece of
paper.
How do you read its reflection?

3   Ask the learners to follow the instructions, carry out the
experiments, and discuss the results in their group. (Answers: A –
The finger has moved to the right. B – The reflection on the other
side of the spoon (concave) has turned upside down. C – The
pupils have become smaller. They get larger in the dark, smaller in
the light. D – The mirror image is touching its left ear. The
reflection of the name in the mirror reads backwards.)

4   Tell the learners that they are going to instruct the other groups
how to do the experiment their group has just carried out. Invite
them to read through the instructions again and remember the
steps. Encourage them to practise saying the instructions.

5   Divide the class into groups of four. Have an A, B, C, and D learner
in each group. Ask the learners to take turns, tell each other what to
do in each experiment, and carry all of them out.

6   While the learners are working in the groups, write the following
sentence frames on the board:

*The pupils get … in the dark. When the light is brighter, they
become …*

The reflection on the concave side of the spoon is …

*When I touch my right ear and look in the mirror, the mirror image
is touching its … ear.*

The reflection of my name in the mirror reads …

The finger lined up with the distant object has moved to the …

7   When the learners finish their experiments, give everyone a sheet of
paper. Ask them to use the sentence frames on the board and write
down the results of the experiments. Check their answers.

16 Pictograms

TARGET LANGUAGE	Past simple
CROSS-CURRICULAR LINKS	Art, Culture studies
MATERIALS	A sheet of paper and a pencil for each learner
PREPARATION	None
TIME GUIDE	45 minutes

Lesson

1 Tell the learners they are going to pretend that they are translators from English into an old Indian language. Explain that many Native American tribes did not have a written alphabet. They used pictures (pictograms) to represent words.

2 Copy the following Native American pictograms on the board. Ask the learners to guess what words they represent (Answers: war, peace, spring, summer, horse, wise).

Ask the learners if they can make a sentence using some or all of the symbols.

3 Divide the class into groups of seven. There can be more people in the group, but not fewer. Tell the learners that they will work on their own and exchange information within their group. It is important that each group member has a fixed seat and does not change it before the activity is over.

4 Give each learner a sheet of paper. Ask them to think of a simple sentence in the Past simple they can write in English. Tell them to write the sentence on the paper.

> *Grandma liked listening to music.*

5 Clockwise, each learner passes the sheet of paper with the sentence to another group member sitting next to him or her. Everyone should have a sheet of paper with someone else's sentence.

6 Tell the learners to read the new sentence and convert it into a picture which represents its meaning. Encourage them to pretend they are translators. Ask them to draw the picture below the sentence. Tell them that there will be five more translators working on the same sheet of paper so it is necessary to be economical and use only 1/6 of the sheet for the drawing.

7 When they finish their drawing, ask them to fold the top of the paper in such a way that the next translator can only see their drawing, not the sentence.

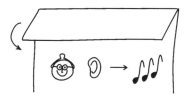

8 Tell the learners to pass the paper clockwise to the next group member as they did before. Now they study the drawing and translate the message from the picture into written English again. Ask the learners to use their imagination and not to worry whether they translate the message exactly the same way it was first written. Just remind them that the sentence is in the Past simple. When the new sentences have been written, the learners fold the paper again. The next translator should only see the sentence.

He had an ear for music.

9 The activity continues in the same pattern. The next translator converts the sentence into a picture, the person after that a picture into a sentence. It is necessary to fold the paper each time. The activity finishes when seven learners have written or drawn on the same sheet of paper. The last translator's step should be writing a sentence. Everyone keeps the paper they wrote on last.

10 Invite the group members to sit together. Ask them to unfold the sheet they are holding and read out to one another the sentences from the paper. The original sentence has most probably been changed in an interesting way.

11 Ask the groups to spread out all their sheets of paper on a desk. Give them time to read them again and choose one or two they would like to share with other groups. Ask the groups to read out the selected texts.

17 The Solar System

TARGET LANGUAGE | Making comparisons
| Colours
CROSS-CURRICULAR LINKS | Science, Art
RESOURCES | The board, a sheet of paper for each learner, coloured pencils
PREPARATION | None
TIME GUIDE | 45 minutes

Lesson

1 Draw a simple picture of the Sun and the Earth on the board as in the picture below. Explain that the Sun is a large star and the Earth is a planet that is much smaller than the Sun. If the Sun were as tall as an adult man, then the Earth would be as small as a grape. Ask the learners what colour the Sun and Earth are. Write the learners' suggestions below the pictures and the names *Sun* and *Earth* above.

2 Give each learner a sheet of paper. Ask them to copy the drawing from the board. Explain that you are going to tell them about the other eight planets of the Solar System. Tell them to follow your description and draw the other planets on the sheet.

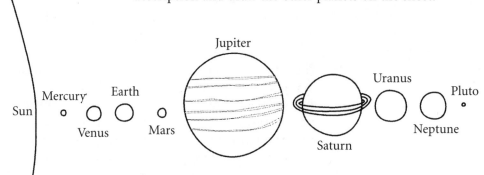

3 As you describe each planet make sure you write its name on the board. The learners can draw in pencil and write a note about each planet's colour in the drawing (or use coloured pencils). Describe the planets in simple sentences. Make gestures to explain and repeat descriptions as necessary. For example:

Venus: Venus is closer to the Sun than the Earth. It's smaller than the Earth, but not much. It's cream-coloured.
Mercury: Mercury is closer to the Sun than Venus. It's the closest planet to the Sun. Mercury is very small. It's smaller than Venus or the Earth. It's the second smallest planet in the Solar system. If you imagine the Earth is like a grape, Mercury is the size of a pea. It looks grey.
Mars: Mars is further from the Sun than the Earth. It's smaller than the Earth, but larger than Mercury. Mars is red.

34

Jupiter: Jupiter is further from the Sun than Mars. It's the largest planet in the Solar system. If we see the Earth as a grape, Jupiter is as big as a grapefruit. It's light-coloured, but there are dark bands on it.

Saturn: Saturn is further from the Sun than Jupiter. It's smaller than Jupiter. It's the second largest planet in the Solar system. If you imagine Jupiter is like a grapefruit, Saturn is the size of an orange. It's yellow. If we use a telescope, we can see it has got three rings.

Uranus: Uranus is further from the Sun than Saturn. It's smaller than Saturn, but much larger than the Earth. If we see Saturn as an orange, Uranus is a lemon. It's blue-green.

Neptune: Neptune is further from the Sun than Uranus. It's almost the size of Uranus, but just a bit smaller. It's still much larger than the Earth. Neptune is blue.

Pluto: Pluto is the furthest planet from the Sun. It's also the smallest in the Solar System. It's smaller than Mercury. In most pictures it looks grey.

4 Let the learners compare their drawings in pairs briefly. Then ask the learners questions about the planets and draw them on the board. For example, 'Is Venus closer to the Sun than the Earth?', 'Is it smaller or larger than the Earth?', 'What colour is it?'.

5 Write the question frames on the board:

Is it closer to ... than ...?   Is it further from ... than ...?

Is it larger than ...?   Is it smaller than ...?

Is it (colour)?

6 Invite one learner to the board and tell him or her to think of one planet from the drawing. Ask questions using the question frames above to learn which one it is. The learner can only answer: 'Yes, it is.' or 'No, it isn't.'

7 Next, you think of one planet from the drawing. This time get the class to ask you questions to learn which planet you are thinking of.

8 Divide the class into pairs. Let them use their pictures and ask and answer questions about the planets as you demonstrated.

18 Sound and hearing

TARGET LANGUAGE 'Sounds' vocabulary area
Animals

CROSS-CURRICULAR LINKS Science, Biology

RESOURCES The board, a sheet of paper and a pencil for each learner

PREPARATION Draw the table from stage 2 on the board without the numbers or letters.

TIME GUIDE 45 minutes

Lesson

1 Explain to the learners that humans can hear low-frequency sounds like a bass drum, and high-frequency sounds like the top note of a recorder or flute. Ask the learners to think of some more examples of high- and low-frequency sounds.

2 Explain that some animals can hear sounds beyond the human range, i.e. low-frequency sounds below 20 hertz and high-frequency sounds beyond 20,000 hertz. Point to the table on the board and ask the learners to if they can guess which animals from the table can hear sounds above or below the human range.

Type of animal	Range of hearing in hertz (approximate)	
Humans	20–20,000	—
Elephants	1–10,000	c
Dolphins	75–150,000	f
Dogs	40–40,000	a
Cats	100–60,000	b
Bats	2,000–120,000	d
Moths	1,000–240,000	e

3 Read the following descriptions of the animals from the chart a few times. Ask the learners to listen and decide which animals are being described and then write down the hearing ranges of the animals in their chart.

a They can hear high-frequency sounds people are not able to detect. That's why they often run and hide when you switch on a vacuum cleaner. It is high frequency sounds we can't hear that are unpleasant for them. People sometimes train these animals to respond to metal whistles that humans themselves don't perceive. Their range of hearing is about 40 to 40,000 hertz.

b These animals can also hear a special ultrasound whistle, but they are too independent to respond to it. They can hear high-frequency squeaks of mice hiding in holes that people can't detect. Their range of hearing is about 100 to 60,000 hertz.

c These animals can make very low-frequency sounds we can't hear. They use them to communicate with their friends that are able to detect such sounds as far as nine kilometres away. A herd of these large mammals can suddenly lift their heads from drinking, bathing, or eating and all look in one direction where humans hear no sound at all. Their range of hearing is about 1 to 10,000 hertz.

d They can detect sounds above the range of human hearing. They use sound waves for navigation. The animal sends ultrasound waves of around 100,000 hertz that bounce off the rocks and trees. They can see and locate their food by how the signal comes back to them. Their range of hearing is about 2,000 to 120,000 hertz.

e Their range of hearing is very wide. They use their hearing ability for protection. When they detect the sound waves of a bat, for example, they dive towards the ground to avoid contact. Their range of hearing is about 1,000 to 240,000 hertz.

f They communicate with each other by whistling at a frequency that people are able to hear. They can also produce ultrasound signals for echolocation. By listening to the echoes of the sound they create, they can locate objects and other fish. Their range of hearing is about 75 to 150,000 hertz.

4 Ask learners to come up to the board, fill in one row of the chart and explain the answer, for example, 'Elephants can hear low frequency sounds between 1 to 10,000 hertz.'

5 Copy this table on the board next to the first table.

Sounds	Frequency (approximate)
a dolphin whistling	4,000–20,000
an elephant calling	14–24
a bat's echolocation	100,000
a rhino calling	5
a cat purring	27–44
a whale's echolocation	20,000–100,000
a mouse squeaking	40,000–70,000
a giraffe calling	14

Put the learners in pairs. Ask them to prepare five quiz questions for another pair using the information from this chart, the chart from stage 2, and the sentence pattern, 'If you were a … , could you hear a …?'. For example, 'If you were an elephant, could you hear a mouse squeaking?'.

19 Musical instruments

TARGET LANGUAGE	'Musical instruments' vocabulary area
CROSS-CURRICULAR LINKS	Music
RESOURCES	The board; household items and materials for making musical instruments, for example: plastic bottles, tins, glass bottles, dry peas, beans or lentils, metal spoons, wooden spoons, small paper boxes, rubber bands, plastic or paper tubes, funnels, combs, tissue paper for stage 1
PREPARATION	Bring the household items and materials for making musical instruments to class.
TIME GUIDE	45 minutes

Lesson

1   Divide the class into groups of four or five. Give each group some household items and materials you brought to class (see 'Resources' above). Ask the groups to use their imagination and make some homemade musical instruments from these materials.

A few ideas for homemade instruments

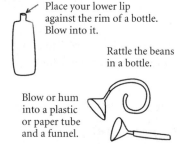

Place your lower lip against the rim of a bottle. Blow into it.

Rattle the beans in a bottle.

Blow or hum into a plastic or paper tube and a funnel.

Strike metal or wooden spoons against each other.

Fill glass bottles with water. Strike them with a spoon.

Place a piece of tissue paper against the side of the comb. Press your lips against the comb and hum.

A string instrument made from a paper box and rubber bands. Play by plucking the bands.

While the learners are working on the instruments, write the following table on the board.

Sections	Strings	Woodwinds	Brass	Percussion
Instruments	violin	oboe	trumpet	drum
	cello	flute	trombone	cymbals
	harp	clarinet	French horn	xylophone
Method of playing	plucking or bowing	blowing	blowing	striking

2   With the help of the chart, introduce the four sections of musical instruments: strings, woodwinds, brass, and percussion. Give examples of instruments that are members of the sections. Demonstrate how these instruments are played, for example, mime plucking or bowing the strings of a violin.

3   Get the learners to think which sections their instruments could be in. Ask them to show and describe to the class how they are played and what real musical instruments they remind them of. For example, 'This is a percussion instrument. I play it by striking the bottles with the metal spoon. It actually reminds me of a xylophone.'

4   Explain to the learners that the four sections of the musical instruments have a fixed sitting arrangement in the orchestra. Discuss which instruments have louder or sharper sounds and which ones sound softer. Let the learners think and talk about how it could influence their sitting arrangement.

5   Draw Picture A on the board and ask the learners questions to elicit where the sections of instruments are traditionally seated in the orchestra. For example, 'Do the strings sit at the back or at the front?', 'Are they positioned to the right or to the left of the conductor?', 'Where do the woodwinds sit?', etc. Write the names of the sections in the plan as you are discussing them with the learners (see Picture B).

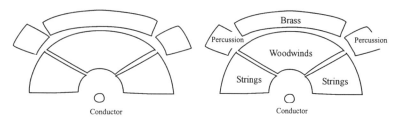

Picture A   Picture B

6   Ask everyone to take one of the instruments they have made in the groups. Tell the learners to divide themselves into the four sections (strings, woodwinds, brass, and percussion) according to the instruments they are holding. Ask them to imagine that the desks and chairs in the classroom represent the orchestra seating. Invite the sections to go and sit in the corresponding parts of the classroom.

7   Pretend that you are a conductor. Invite each section to play their instruments together for a little while. Use your imagination and combine interesting sounds. Invite a few instruments from different sections to play together.

Variation
Ask the learners in each section to play together and prepare a 'musical composition' to perform for the other groups.

20 Weight

TARGET LANGUAGE   Metric and non-metric weight units
Calculations
Making suggestions and expressing opinions

CROSS-CURRICULAR LINKS   Mathematics

RESOURCES   The board, a pencil and a sheet of paper for each learner

PREPARATION   Write the list for stage 1 on the board.

TIME GUIDE   45 minutes

Lesson

1   Ask the learners to imagine that they are going for an afternoon hike. They are taking a train to get out of town and walk in the countryside for a few hours. Point to the list and tell the learners that they are going to decide which things from the list they want to take with them. Each learner will be carrying a backpack that can only hold 3 kilograms.

sandwich	220g	apple	8oz
bottle of water	1kg	chocolate bar	15g
pen	8g	notebook	5oz
camera	9oz	hat	60g
map	2oz	compass	70g
penknife	50g	purse/wallet	200g
first aid kit	1lb	book	250g
sunglasses	20g	raincoat	3lb

2   Explain that the weight of the objects in the list is given in different units of measurement. Gram (g) and kilogram (kg) are metric measures (1000g = 1kg), ounce (oz) and pound (lb) are non-metric (1lb = 16oz). Explain how the learners can convert the units (Answer: 1lb = 454g, 1oz = 28.35g).

3   Give everyone a sheet of paper and a pencil. Divide the class into groups of four. Ask the groups to rearrange the items in the list from the lightest to the heaviest converting the weight of the items into metric units.

4   Invite one of the groups to read out the list arranged from the lightest to the heaviest item. Check it with the help of the other groups. (Answers: Pen 8g, chocolate bar 15g, sunglasses 20g, penknife 50g, map approx. 57g, hat 60g, compass 70g, notebook approx. 142g, purse/wallet 200g, sandwich 220 g, apple approx. 227g, book 250g, camera approx. 255g, first aid kit approx 454g, a bottle of water 1000g, raincoat approx. 1361g.)

5 Write the following sentence frames on the board:

I'd like to take …　　　　　　　*That's a good idea.*
I think … is useful.　　　　　　*I agree.*
Do we need two …?　　　　　　*I'm not sure.*
Why don't we take …?
Let's take …

6 Divide the class into pairs. Tell the pairs that the two of them are going to share one backpack on the hike. Remind them that it can only hold 3kg. Invite the pairs to use the sentence frames from the board to compare their lists and agree on what they are going to pack for the hike in the same luggage. Encourage the learners to use the language of maths as they carry out the calculations. For example:

70g + 220g = 290g　　　　seventy grams **plus** two hundred and twenty grams **equals/is** two hundred and ninety grams

3000g − 454g = 2546g　　Three thousand grams **minus** four hundred and fifty-four grams **makes** two thousand five hundred and forty-six grams.

Ask them to write down their new list.

7 Divide the class into groups of four from the pairs. This time the four of them are going to share the same backpack. Let the group discuss what they should take with them for the hike. Tell them to write a list of the items the four of them agreed to pack for the hike.

8 Invite the groups to read out their lists. How do the lists compare? Are they similar or different? Ask the groups to exchange their lists, add up the weight of all the items in the list, and check if the total is below 3kg.

21 Library

TARGET LANGUAGE	'Literature' vocabulary area Nationalities
CROSS-CURRICULAR LINKS	Literature
RESOURCES	The board, a sheet of paper and a pencil for each learner, paper cards, sellotape
PREPARATION	Make the cards for stage 1: six cards, one for each author's name, labelled 1–6; six cards with details about the author and book, labelled a–f. The cards shown are examples. Choose authors and books that are suitable and interesting for your class.
TIME GUIDE	45 minutes

Lesson

1 Stick the cards on the wall so that they are in a random order. Give all the learners a sheet of paper and a pencil and invite them to walk around and read the text on the cards. Ask them to discuss the information in pairs or threes and match the names of the writers with the details.

Authors' names
1 Miguel de Cervantes　　4 Antoine de Saint-Exupéry
2 L.M. Montgomery　　　5 J.K. Rowling
3 Karen Blixen　　　　　6 Karel Čapek

Details

a A Danish novelist, born in Copenhagen in 1885. She lived on a coffee plantation in Africa for almost 20 years. She wrote a book about her life in Kenya called 'Out of Africa'. In 1985 the book was made into an Oscar-winning film.

b A French writer and pilot, born in Lyon in 1900. In 1920s and 1930s he flew mail across the Sahara Desert to South African cities. He wrote 'The Little Prince', a story about a small boy from another planet and a pilot who meet in the desert.

c A Czech novelist, short-story writer, and dramatist, born in 1890. Together with his brother Josef, he invented the word 'robot'. He first used the word in his play 'R.U.R.' about artificial human beings.

d An English children's author, born in 1965. When sitting on a delayed train from Manchester to London in 1990, she had an idea to write a story about a wizard boy. In 1997 she published the first Harry Potter book. Her books have been translated into more than 30 languages.

e A Canadian novelist, born in 1874 on Prince Edward Island. She wrote 'Anne of Green Gables' about a redheaded orphan girl. Each year thousands of visitors travel to Prince Edward Island to see Green Gables House, the setting of her novel.

f A Spanish novelist and dramatist, born in 1547. He was a contemporary of William Shakespeare. He wrote 'Don Quixote', which is often called the first modern novel. The main character, Don Quixote, is an idealistic knight of La Mancha who seeks adventure.

2 Check the answers (1–f, 2–e, 3–a, 4–b, 5–d, 6–c). Remove the cards from the wall and stick them on the board. Ask the learners whether they know these authors or their works. Explain any vocabulary the learners are not familiar with.

3 Write these substitution tables on the board:

What's the name of the	*English*	*novelist*	*who wrote ...?*
	French	*dramatist*	
	Spanish	*short-story writer*	
	Canadian	*children's author*	
	American	*poet*	

What's the title of the	*book*	*about ...?*
	novel	*by ...?*
	play	
	poem	

4 Pretend that you are in a library looking for a book, but you do not remember its title or author. Give the learners some hints about what you are looking for. Get them to use the information from the cards and give you the name or title. For example, 'Excuse me, I'm looking for a book. What's the title of the novel about the girl living on Prince Edward Island? / What's the title of the book by Karen Blixen? / What's the name of the children's author who wrote the Harry Potter series?'

5 Divide the class into pairs. Invite the learners to ask each other questions about the authors or their works as you demonstrated in stage 4.

6 Ask the learners to think about their favourite books, short stories, plays, or poems. Invite them to use the language from the substitution charts to prepare two questions about the authors or books they like. For example, 'What's the name of the Swedish children's author who wrote the stories about Pippi Longstocking?'; 'What's the title of the play by G.B. Shaw about a flower girl who learns to speak like a lady?'.

7 Invite the learners to ask their two questions to ten other learners in the class. Tell them to write down a point for each correct answer they get. Check how many points they have counted. Which title or author were the learners most familiar with?

22 Maps

TARGET LANGUAGE	'Maps' vocabulary area Question forms and short answers Giving directions
CROSS-CURRICULAR LINKS	Geography
RESOURCES	The board, a sheet of paper and a pencil for each learner
PREPARATION	Draw the grid, compass, and boxes from stage 1 on the board.
TIME GUIDE	45 minutes

Lesson

1 Point at the grid and explain to the learners that it represents a map of an area outside the town/city where you are teaching. If they ask you questions and arrange the boxes in the grid like pieces of a jigsaw puzzle, they can learn what the place looks like.

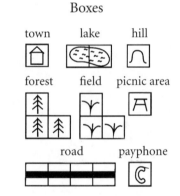

2 Draw the town in the empty grid as a starting point. Explain to the learners that they can move horizontally, vertically, or diagonally in the grid. If they move vertically or horizontally, they use kilometers to specify the distance. If they move diagonally, they refer to the distance in squares. Write the substitution table on the board:

Is there a ...	one two three	kilometre kilometres	north of the ...? west of the ...? south of the ...? east of the ...?
Is there a ...	one two three	square squares	north-east of the ...? north-west of the ...? south-east of the ...? south-west of the ...?

3 Demonstrate how the learners can ask questions, for example, 'Is there a forest one kilometre east of the town?', 'Is there a forest two kilometers north of the town?', 'Is there a forest one square north-east of the town?'. You only answer 'Yes, there is.' or 'No, there isn't.'.

Picture A

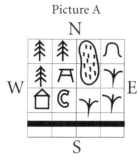

Picture B

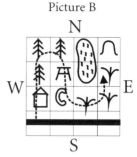

4   Give each learner a sheet of paper and a pencil. Ask them to copy the grid from the board. Invite them to take turns and ask you questions about the map. Use the map from Picture A to answer their questions. Encourage the learners to listen to all the questions and answers carefully and draw the map in their grid.

5   When they have completed the map, ask the learners questions about it, for example, 'What's three kilometres east of the town?', 'What's one square south-east of the town?' 'Is there a hill north of the payphone?' With their help, draw the map on the board.

6   Say that now, when they have the map, you can tell them exactly where you went for a walk and where you took a photo. Tell the learners to start in the square south of the town. Ask them to follow your directions and draw the route in their map. Give directions and pause to give the learners some time to think and draw. For example:

> First, go three kilometres north. Then turn and go one kilometre east. There you turn south and go for two more kilometres. Next, go two kilometres east. And finally, turn and go one kilometre north. That's the place where I stopped, turned west and took a picture. What do you think was in the photo?
> (Answer: The lake and the forest with the picnic area in the background.)

7   Get the learners to give you the directions back and draw the route on the board. (See Picture B in stage 3).

8   Ask the learners to draw two empty grids (the same size as before) on their sheets. The first one is for their own map. Invite them to use the boxes with the pictures from the board, arrange them in the grid in another way, and create a new map. You can also ask them to mark a route of a walk there.

9   Divide the class into pairs. Tell the pairs not to show each other their maps, but ask questions like they did in the whole class activity and draw their partner's map in the second grid. You can organize it as a competition. The one in the pair who draws the partner's map first is a winner. Let them compare their drawings when they finish. The learners also give each other directions to draw the route.

23 Materials

TARGET LANGUAGE   'Materials' vocabulary area
                  Adjectives to describe materials
                  It's made of …, It's too …, It isn't … enough.

CROSS-CURRICULAR LINKS   Science

RESOURCES   The board, a sheet of paper and a pencil for each learner, a big
            non-transparent plastic bag

PREPARATION   Bring objects made of different materials to the class (at least one
              object for each pair of learners). Write the text from stage 5 on the
              board.
              Avoid using things that could hurt the learners.

TIME GUIDE   45–50 minutes

Lesson

1   Show the learners the objects you have brought to the class and
    introduce the materials they are made of. Write the expressions on
    the board. For example:

    wood   metal   cloth   plastic   glass
    stone   wax   rubber   paper   clay

2   With the help of the objects, teach the learners the adjectives they
    could use to describe the quality of the materials. Write the words
    on the board. For example:

    soft   hard   heavy   light   transparent
    elastic   waterproof   warm   fragile   strong

3   Divide the class into pairs. Give each pair an object made of one of
    the materials you introduced in stage 1. Avoid using things that
    could hurt the learners. Ask them to read through the list of
    adjectives on the board and decide which adjectives can be used to
    describe the quality of the material their object is made of. For
    example: glass – smooth, heavy, transparent, fragile; rubber – soft,
    light, elastic, waterproof; stone – hard, heavy, strong.

4   Tell the learners to hide the objects in their pockets, wrap them up
    in their sweaters or hold them behind their backs so that other
    pairs cannot see them. Ask them to walk in the classroom, describe
    the qualities of the material their object is made of to other pairs,
    and let them guess which material it is. When the other pair have
    made a guess, they can show them the object.

5   Write the following sentence patterns on the board:

    Why isn't/aren't … made of …?
    Because … is too …
    Because … isn't … enough.

6 Ask the class a few questions about why certain things or objects are not made of certain materials. Get the learners to use the sentence patterns from the board to answer them. For example:

Wax bridges: Why aren't bridges made of wax? – Because wax isn't strong enough / is too soft.

Stone pillows: Why aren't pillows made of stone? – Because stone is too hard and heavy / isn't soft or light enough.

Paper sweaters: Why aren't sweaters made of paper? – Because paper isn't strong or elastic enough.

7 Ask the learners to think about other unusual or funny combinations of objects and materials. Give everyone a sheet of paper and tell the learners to write their ideas down.

8 Invite the learners to stand up and walk around the classroom. Tell them to ask their questions about why the objects in their lists are not made of the particular materials to as many learners as possible and listen to their answers. When the activity is over, invite the class to share the most interesting questions they remember they were asked.

Variation 1
Divide the class into two groups, A and B. Ask the learners to imagine they are part of a phone-in radio programme. The As are listeners and the Bs are experts. Ask the As to take turns and 'phone in' their questions. Get the Bs to take turns and answer them. You can use, for example, two pencils as props. One pencil as a telephone receiver for the As to pass on and the other one as a microphone for the Bs. Then switch the roles.

Variation 2
Ask the learners to write their question on a piece of paper and fold it. Prepare a plastic bag and ask the learners to put their folded strips in it. Mix the pieces of paper in the bag. Let individual learners pull a question out of the bag, read it out and answer it.

Follow-up
Practise using the structure, 'It's made of …'. Put the objects you have brought to use in stages 1–4 in the plastic bag. Hold the bag. Invite individual learners to come to the board, put their hands in the bag, feel one of the objects and say what it is made of. You can also ask them to describe the material using the adjectives from stage 2 before they pull the object out of the bag.

24 Tree rings

TARGET LANGUAGE   Past passive
Time expressions
'Inventions and discoveries' vocabulary area

CROSS-CURRICULAR LINKS   History, Science, Biology

RESOURCES   The board, a sheet of paper and a pencil for each learner
Two posters for stage 6:

Poster A
1895   A film was first shown in public.
1896   Toothpaste in a tube was first sold.
1898   Radium was discovered.
1899   The paperclip was invented.
1903   The first airplane was flown.

Poster B
1867   Dynamite was invented.
1869   Chewing gum was first sold.
1874   DNA was discovered.
1876   The telephone was invented.
1878   The first light bulb was made.

PREPARATION   Draw the tree ring from stage 1 on the board.
Prepare the posters for stage 6. You can make these easier or more
difficult depending on your class.

TIME GUIDE   45 minutes

Lesson

1   Ask the class to guess how old the oldest tree is. (Answer: Bristlecone pines, native to the Rocky Mountains of the United States, which are about 4,700 years old.) Point to the picture of the tree rings on the board and explain that the rings on the stump show us how the tree grew. Each dark ring together with the light inner layer count as one year. Ask the learners to count the dark rings on the stump to learn how old the tree was when it was cut down (13 years old for this tree).

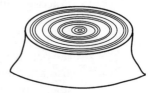

2   Tell the learners to imagine that the tree was cut down this year (the activity works with 2003 as an example). Count back the rings and get the learners to say which year each ring stands for. For example: 'This is a year ago, it's 2002 (two thousand and two). This is four years ago, it's 1999 (nineteen ninety-nine).'

3 Draw five arrows pointing at some dark rings in the picture on the board.

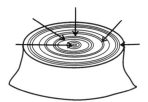

4 Invite the learners to imagine that the tree was cut down in 1688. Ask them to calculate which five years the arrows indicate. Get them to tell you the years indicated by the arrows (Answers: 1676, 1679, 1681, 1682, 1687).

5 Write the question frame on the board: *What happened in …?*. Get the learners to ask you questions about what happened in those years and answer them using these notes:

1676 Lemonade was first sold in Paris.
1679 The pressure cooker was invented.
1681 A tunnel was first made with the help of gunpowder.
1682 The building of the Palace of Versailles was finished. King Louis XIV moved in.
1687 Gravity was discovered by Newton.

6 Give each learner a sheet of paper and a pencil. Divide the class in half. Ask one group to come to the front of the classroom and the other one to gather at the back. Place the two posters, A at the front and B at the back, on the floor. Ask the learners to copy the years and events from the poster.

7 Give everyone another sheet of paper. Tell them to draw a stump with 12 tree rings on the paper. Ask them to draw an arrow pointing at the largest dark ring and write the last year from their list of years and events next to it (1903 for A, 1878 for B). Then tell them to mark other years from their list on the rings with arrows. Ask them not to write any numbers for the rest of the arrows.

8 Pair up the learners from the two groups. Let each pair exchange the sheets of paper with the rings and arrows. Ask them to calculate which years the arrows are pointing at.

9 Tell the learners to take turns and ask each other questions about what happened in those years and write down the answers next to the arrows. Let them compare their sentences when they have finished.

Follow up
Invite the learners to design and draw their own tree rings about events and changes in their town/city, country, or the world.

25 Pulse

TARGET LANGUAGE   Past simple
Numbers

CROSS-CURRICULAR LINKS   Biology, Maths, Physical education

RESOURCES   The board, a watch with a second hand or a stopwatch, a sheet of paper and a pencil for each learner

PREPARATION   Practise taking your pulse.

TIME GUIDE   45 minutes

Lesson

1   Explain or mime the word 'heartbeat', for example, by beating your fist on your chest. Ask the learners where on the human body they can feel their pulse. (Answer: It can be felt on the inside part of the wrist below the thumb or on the neck under the jaw.) Show the places on your wrist and neck. Encourage the learners to find their own pulse.

2   Tell the learners they are going to take their own pulse and do some simple calculations. Do the measurement together with the learners, giving and demonstrating the simple instructions below. Invite the learners to follow you. Write your results on the board as an example.

Instructions

TEACHER   *Place your fingers on your wrist below the thumb or under the jaw on your neck.*

(Make sure everyone can feel their pulse.)

Count the beats you feel for 15 seconds.

Start.

(Wait 15 seconds.)

Stop.

Write down the number you have counted. (For example 19 beats.)

Multiply the number of beats you counted by 4.

Write an example calculation on the board: 19 x 4 = 76 beats a minute. Explain that this is the number of times your heart beats in one minute.

3 Ask a few learners what their pulse is. Tell the learners to walk around the classroom and ask each other what their pulse is. If they find someone with the same pulse rate as theirs, they should write down his or her name. Check how many names the learners have in their lists at the end of the activity.

4 Draw a chart with a list of activities on the board, for example:

Activity	Name	Pulse
walking		
doing sit-ups		
doing press-ups		
jogging		
running on the spot		
sitting cross-legged and breathing deeply		
doing a stretching exercise		
lifting weights		

Ask the class which activities they think will make their pulse the highest and lowest.

5 Put the learners into pairs and tell them to choose two activities from the list. They should then do the activity for one minute and at the end take the other person's pulse. When they have all finished, tell them to walk around the class asking other people what their pulse was for the same or different activities and write the results and names in the table. For example,

LEARNER 1   *What activity did you do?*
LEARNER 2   *I jogged for a minute.*
LEARNER 1   *What was your pulse at the end?*
LEARNER 2   *It was 110 beats a minute.*

6 When they have finished collecting results, tell everyone to work with their original partner and order the activities from highest to lowest pulse. Go through the results with the whole class.

26 Fruit and vegetables

TARGET LANGUAGE	'Fruit and vegetables' vocabulary area Talking about future plans
CROSS-CURRICULAR LINKS	Biology, Geography
RESOURCES	The board; a sheet of paper and a pencil for each learner
PREPARATION	Draw the picture of a garden, garden tools, and vegetable seeds from stage 1 and write the list of garden activities from stage 2 on the board. Practise miming the garden activities from stage 2.
TIME GUIDE	40 minutes

Lesson

1 Point to the picture on the board and ask the class to imagine that it is a garden they are going to look after for one year. Describe the garden in simple sentences. Explain that there are two fruit trees, apple and cherry, and three vegetable beds. Point out that there is also a lawn under the trees they are going to look after. Tell the learners about the garden tools. Point at each tool, and mime or describe what they are used for, for example, 'The rake is for raking the leaves.'

apple tree   cherry tree

Seeds

cucumbers radishes

tomatoes carrots

peas onions

Tools

rake

hoe

watering can

mower

2 Read through the list of garden activities and explain the words the learners do not understand. Then invite the learners to read them out with you.

Mow the grass.   *Water the seeds.*
Pull the weeds.   *Clean the tools.*
Water the garden.   *Harvest the fruit and vegetables.*
Plant the vegetables.   *Hoe the vegetable beds.*

3 Choose one activity from the list and mime it. Let the learners guess which activity it is. Ask a few learners to mime some activities from the list for others to guess.

4 Give each learner a sheet of paper. Ask them to decide on their own when they are going to do the activities in their garden. Write *Spring, Summer, Autumn*, and *Winter* on the board. Tell the learners to divide the garden activities into these four groups on their sheets. They can do the same activity in more than one season if they want to.

5 Tell the learners to decide which vegetables they are going to grow. Read through the vegetable vocabulary on the left side of the picture. Ask the learners to choose three kinds of vegetables and write their choice down on their sheets.

6 Write the following sentence patterns on the board:

What are you going to grow? – I'm going to grow …

When are you going to …? – I'm going to … in the spring/summer/autumn/winter.

7 Divide the learners into pairs. Pair up learners who do not sit at the same desk. Tell the pairs not to show each other their notes, but use the sentence frames from the board to ask each other about their plans for the garden. Encourage them to listen and compare the plans. Tell them to count a point for each same vegetable they are going to grow and for each activity they both listed in the same season. For example:

LEARNER 1 *What are you going to grow?*
LEARNER 2 *I'm going to grow carrots, cucumbers, and onions.*
LEARNER 1 *I'm going to grow cucumbers, tomatoes, and radishes.*
LEARNER 2 *When are you going to hoe the vegetable beds?*
LEARNER 1 *I'm going to do it in the summer.*

8 Check how many points the pairs have at the end of the activity. Which pairs have the most points?

9 There is no one right way of dividing the garden activities into seasons. Some activities, however, are more typical of some seasons than others, for example, planting the vegetables – spring, watering the seeds – spring, mowing the grass – summer, harvesting the fruit and vegetables – summer and autumn, raking the old leaves – autumn. Go through the list of garden activities again. Ask a few learners about each activity to see how different or similar their plans are.

27 Voice

TARGET LANGUAGE 'Voice' vocabulary area
Consonant sounds – /p/, /m/, /f/, etc.

CROSS-CURRICULAR LINKS Biology

RESOURCES The board, a sheet of paper and a pencil for each learner

PREPARATION Make the posters for stage 1 and put them on the wall at the opposite ends of the classroom.
Write the instructions for stage 2 on the board.
Draw Picture A from stage 4 on the board. Try making the sounds from stage 5 yourself before the class.

TIME GUIDE 45 minutes

Lesson

1 Divide the class into two groups, A and B, tell them to look at their poster on the wall, and copy it down.

Group A *The happy little pig met a nice thin frog.*
Group B *The nice happy frog met a thin little pig.*

2 Read the instructions from the board and demonstrate them. Ask the learners to find someone from another group and dictate the sentences from stage 1 to each other following one of the instructions. They should try each instruction once.

Instructions:

a *Hold your nose with your fingers and speak.*
b *Open your mouth and speak without moving your lips.*
c *Speak without moving your tongue. You can hold it with your handkerchief.*
d *Move your lips and tongue, but don't make any sounds.*

3 When they have all said their sentences using the four instructions, ask them if they could understand each other, and if not, why not. (Answer: We need to use our lips, tongue, nose and mouth, and air from our lungs to make sounds.)

4   Point to Picture A on the board and explain to the learners that the picture shows the parts of the body we use when we speak. Elicit the words to describe the body parts the learners already know and teach the ones that are new. Label the picture (see Picture B).

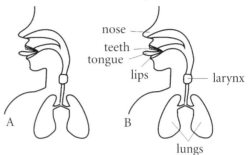

5   Draw the following grid on the board (without the ticks). Ask the learners to copy it.

	The lips are closed.	The lips open and air comes out.	The lower lip touches the teeth.	The tongue touches the teeth.	The tongue moves inside the mouth.	The air goes through the mouth.	The air goes through the nose.
/p/		✓					
/l/				✓	✓		
/m/	✓						✓
/f/			✓			✓	
/θ/ (<u>th</u>ink)				✓	✓		
/n/							✓
/h/						✓	

6   Ask the learners to put a small piece of paper on the palm of their hand and say the consonant /p/ so that the paper flies off their hand. Ask them how they made the sound and chose a box in the chart.

7   Ask the learners to work on their own. Tell them to say the consonants in the first column and observe how they produce the sounds. Ask them to tick all relevant boxes in the grid to record their answers.

8   Divide the class into groups of four. Ask the learners to say the sounds again, observe each other's mouths, and compare their notes. Give each group a new consonant – /b/, /v/, /k/, and /g/ and ask them to describe what they do with their lips, teeth, and tongues. When they have finished, go through the answers together.

28 Timetable

TARGET LANGUAGE	Numbers in time expressions Talking about future plans
CROSS-CURRICULAR LINKS	Maths, Life skills
RESOURCES	The board, a pencil and a sheet of paper for each learner
PREPARATION	Write the 'To do' list from stage 2 on the board. The type of currency is optional.
TIME GUIDE	45 minutes

Lesson

1   Tell the learners that they have been invited to their best friend's birthday party which starts at five o'clock. They get home from school or work at four and have exactly one hour to get ready and get to the party. They have a budget of £20.

2   Point to the 'To do' list on the board and explain that they need to make decisions about what they are going to buy, how much to spend, and the order they are going to do things in, so that they arrive on time and are within budget.

To do	Time (minutes)	Cost (in pounds/£)
take a shower	10	
wrap the present	3	
watch your favourite TV programme	30	
feed the cat	5	
write the birthday card	2	
iron your dress or shirt	5	
clean your shoes	2	
get dressed	5	
buy a birthday present:	20	
some flowers		£11
a CD		£13.50
a box of chocolates		£9
buy a birthday card	10	£4, £3, or £1.50
or make a card	20	£0
get to the party: by taxi	5	£10
on foot	30	£0
by bus	15	£2

3   Ask the learners to work in pairs and look at the different options they have: when to do things, things they are not going to do, things they can do at the same time, how much to spend, etc. They should: decide on a schedule, calculate the total amount of time it will take to get ready (no longer than 60 minutes), and the total amount they are going to spend (no more than £20).

4 Write these sentence patterns on the board:

I'm going to (action) at (time).

First I'm going to (action).

Then I'm going to (action).

At the same time I'm going to (action).

Ask some pairs to tell you some of the things they are going to do.

5 Ask the learners to change partners and describe what they are going to do before the party. The person listening should write down the schedule, time, and budget to make sure their new partner is on target.

Explain to the learners how to read numbers in their timetable and talk about money. For example:

4:00–4:05   'from four to four oh five' (or 'five past four')
4:19–4:21   'from four nineteen to four twenty-one' or 'nineteen
            minutes past four to twenty-one minutes past four'.
£11.00   'eleven pounds'
£1.50   'one fifty' or 'one pound fifty'.

6 Invite pairs to come to the front of the class and mime their plans. The rest of class should describe the plans using 'going to'.

29 Touch, taste, and smell

TARGET LANGUAGE	The 'five senses' vocabulary area **It feels/tastes/smells** + adjective **It feels like a** + noun
CROSS-CURRICULAR LINKS	Science
RESOURCES	The board, a pencil and a sheet of paper for each learner, a non-transparent plastic bag, a selection of different objects to use in stages 1 and 2, samples of different tastes, food or their containers for stages 4 and 5, samples of different smells for stage 10.
PREPARATION	Draw the pictures from **Taste** stage 2 on the board.
TIME GUIDE	45 minutes

Lesson

Touch

1 Write the following adjectives on the board:

thin   thick   rough   smooth   dry   wet

cold   warm   sharp   round   solid   hollow

2 Place a few objects in a non-transparent plastic bag, for example, a piece of wet sponge, a pencil, a pebble, a piece of dried fruit, a cup, etc. Invite a few learners to feel an object in the bag and guess what it is. Write the following sentence patterns on the board:

It feels ...

It feels like a ...

Get the learners to use the sentence patterns to describe the objects. For example, 'It feels smooth, round, and hollow. It feels like a cup.'

3 Divide the class into pairs, A and B. Ask the As to close their eyes. No peeking! Tell the Bs to take their hands, walk them very carefully around the classroom and let them touch different things. Tell them not to use the objects that could hurt them. Ask the As to feel the objects the Bs allow them to touch and describe what they feel like. Then ask the learners to change their roles.

Taste

1 Introduce 'sweet', 'salty', 'sour', and 'bitter'. Bring some samples of these tastes into class if you can and let the learners taste them. For example: sugar (sweet), crisps (salty), lemon (sour), tea with no sugar (bitter).

2 Draw the pictures of the following items of food on the board or use real items of food or their containers (honey, yoghurt, peanuts, chocolate, coffee, olives, strawberries, cheese, pickles, ice cream).

3 Ask the learners to imagine they want to buy some food. However, they cannot remember what the food they want is called. So they have to explain to the shop assistant what it tastes like and describe it in as much detail as they can. Encourage them to use the adjectives they have learned earlier.

4 Write the following dialogue pattern on the board to help them:

Learner 1 I'm sorry. I can't remember what it's called. It tastes ... It's ...

Learner 2 Oh, you mean ...?

5 Ask the learners to get back to their pairs. The As are customers and the Bs shop assistants. Tell the As to describe one item of food from the picture in stage 2. Ask the Bs to guess which food the customer wants to buy. Tell them to change their roles and take turns in describing other items of food.

Smell

1 Bring some samples of interesting smells into class, for example: spices, clean laundry, an old book, vinegar, perfume, etc. Let the learners sniff them and describe their smell. Introduce a few adjectives describing different smells, for example, 'It smells fresh/old/dirty/wonderful/good/bad/terrible.'

2 Write the following words on the board:

onion, Christmas trees, peppermint tea, cigarettes, soap, blue cheese, clean T-shirts, perfume, socks left for 6 months in a gym locker, flowers

Give everyone a sheet of paper and a pencil. Ask them to write 'fresh', 'old', 'dirty', 'wonderful', 'good', 'bad', and 'terrible' on their sheets. Tell the learners to divide the words from the board into these groups according to their smell.

3 Ask the learners to work in pairs again. Invite them to speak about the items in the list, express their opinions about their smell, and compare them with their partner's notes. Ask them to underline the words they disagreed about in their opinions. For example:

LEARNER 1 *Christmas trees smell fresh and wonderful.*
LEARNER 2 *Yes, they do.*
LEARNER 1 *Blue cheese smells terrible.*
LEARNER 2 *Does it? I think it smells good.*

30 Framed pictures

TARGET LANGUAGE   Present continuous
Prepositions of place

CROSS-CURRICULAR LINKS   Drama, Art

RESOURCES   The board; props, for example, a towel, a comb, an umbrella, a hat, two chairs

PREPARATION   The choice of painting is important. The painting in this unit is just one example. The number of characters and the type of scene should be suitable for your class.
Practise describing the painting from stage 2 in simple sentences.

TIME GUIDE   45 minutes

Lesson

1   Ask the class what their favourite painting or photograph is and ask them to describe it – the people, the objects, the background, etc.

2   Tell them that you are going to describe your favourite painting. Ask for five volunteers and tell them they are five characters from the painting. Make sure each of them knows which character you want them to represent. Ask them to mime what the characters are doing. Give the five actors the props: a towel, a comb, an umbrella, a hat, and two chairs, that they can use to make the scene they are going to create look real. Describe the imaginary painting in simple sentences, for example:

> In the painting 'Beach Scene' a girl is lying on a towel. A woman is sitting next to her. She has a comb. The woman is combing the girl's hair. On the right a man and a woman are talking. They are sitting in chairs. The woman is holding an umbrella. The man is holding a hat. On the left a boy is swimming …

3   Ask the actors to stay in their positions for a moment. Point at them and ask the learners a few questions about them. For example, 'What is she doing?', 'What is he holding?'.

4   Encourage the learners to imagine they are artists who are going to paint a picture they want to call 'Summer's Day'. Ask them to think about what people like doing on a summer day. Help with vocabulary or ideas, if necessary. Write their suggestions on the board, for example:

eating ice cream	*reading a book*	*swimming*
drinking water	*wearing sunglasses*	*riding a bicycle*
rowing a boat	*writing a letter*	*fishing*

5 Divide the class into groups of four. Ask each group to work together and create a scene on a summer's day that an artist would find interesting to paint. Each member of the group should decide what he or she is going to do in the scene. They should also make sure the scene works well as a whole. Invite them to use their own ideas or the ideas from the board. Encourage them to make their scene special.

6 When each group has prepared their scene, ask the groups, one after another, to perform it. Work with the class. Ask them to describe what the characters are doing. Encourage the use of the Present continuous. Get some feedback from the authors of the scene to check if the description was correct.

7 At the end of the lesson ask the students to look for the pictures of the paintings of people that they like and could describe. They may have art books at home or borrow them from the school library. Ask them to bring the pictures to the next lesson if they can. Invite them to show the pictures to each other and talk about them.

Variation 1

Do stage 6 as a writing exercise. Have one group perform their scene and ask others to write down the description. For example: *Petra is sitting on a chair. Martin is reading a book. Jana is eating an ice cream.* Let them compare the descriptions in pairs first, then check with the help of the performers.

Variation 2

Invite two groups at the same time. Ask them to line up in front of the board – one group on the left, the other one on the right. Stand in between them. Ask them not to watch the other group, but look straight in front of them at the class. The group on the right performs their scene. The class describes what they are doing. Following the description, the group on the left tries to copy the other group's scene. Compare the two scenes. Then ask the group on the left to perform.